NEWSPAPER REPORTERS

AN INTRODUCTION TO NEWSPAPER WRITING

Written by Marzella Brown

Edited by Sharon Coan

Illustrated by Blanca Apodaca

Teacher Created Materials, Inc.
6421 Industry Way
Westminster, CA 92683
www.teachercreated.com
©1990 Teacher Created Materials, Inc.
Reprinted, 2001
Made in U.S.A.
ISBN 1-55734-137-0

TABLE OF CONTENTS

INTRODUCTION 3
USING THE BOOK 3
PRODUCING A NEWSPAPER

The Newspaper Staff 4
The News Department 5
The News Section 6
The Editorial Section 7
The Feature Section 8
The Sports Section 9
The Entertainment Section 10
Photography 11
Newspaper Art 12
The Business Department—Circulation Section 13
Advertising 14
Classified Advertising 15
The Mechanical Department—Typesetting 16
Layout 17
Layout (cont.) 18
Printing 19
Using The Index 20
Be A Newspaper Detective! 21
Reading Weather Maps 22

WRITING FOR A NEWSPAPER

Writing News Stories 23
A Reporter's Best Friends 24
Find The Facts 25
Taking Notes 26
Writing Leads 27
The Whole Story 28
On Your Own 29
Proofreading 30
Proofreading (cont.) 31
Headlines 32
From The Horse's Mouth 33
The Key To Interviews 34
Direct Quotes 35
Guidelines For Interviews 36
Editorials 37
Types Of Editorials 38
Editorial Cartoons 39
Writing Sports Stories 40
Writing Feature Articles 41
Writing Reviews 42
Comics 43
Puzzles 44
Preparing Advertisements 45
Wonderful Words 46
Practice Assignments 47

ANSWER KEY 48

INTRODUCTION

EXTRA! EXTRA! LEARN ALL ABOUT THE NEWSPAPER

Newspaper Reporters is a sensational new 48 page language arts resource designed to excite students in grades 3-6 about reading and writing by using the newspaper. Students will learn how a newspaper is produced and how to write the various types of newspaper articles.

The lessons and hands-on activities of the first section are designed to help students understand how a newspaper is run and produced. To illustrate the lessons, students are directed to find specific items in a daily newspaper. (These may be given as homework assignments.) They also complete exercises requiring them to differentiate between fact and opinion, to research topics for features, to read a movie schedule, to prepare newspaper art, to make decisions, and more.

Then students are challenged to become reporters as they conduct interviews, do the background research, and use the 5 W's and How to organize note taking and write lead sentences. They will continue on to write their own articles and headlines using the inverted pyramid form for news and sports stories and other styles for editorials, features, and reviews. Students will also prepare comics, puzzles, and ads as they complete their survey of newspaper writing.

In addition, activities designed to increase vocabulary, teach proofreading skills, use an index, etc. improve general language arts skills. With activities that extend into other curriculum areas—science (weather), math (purchasing papers), social studies (career awareness), art (printing), etc.—*Newspaper Reporters* could be used as the central resource for a whole language thematic unit. This versatile book is a must for middle grade teachers!

USING THE BOOK

Teachers may wish to have their students keep a scrapbook into which they will put the items they collect from newspapers and the projects they produce as part of the lessons. The vocabulary-increasing activity suggested on page 46 may be introduced early in the unit and entries made into this scrapbook. A field trip to a local newspaper, if possible, would be an enlivening addition to the unit.

Students should be given the opportunity to produce a newspaper. Teacher Created Materials publishes sets of four page, realistic newspapers (TCM138, *Newspapers*) which allow students to insert their own articles, art, ads, etc. These can be purchased in sets of 15 so that individuals or small groups can create and proudly display their very own paper.

THE NEWSPAPER STAFF

Producing a newspaper is a big job. In a large newspaper the work is divided among departments.

PUBLISHER: Head of the paper. Decides which department will do what work.

NEWS DEPARTMENT: Provides the news, editorial, feature and sports articles, illustrations, and photographs which fill the pages of the newspaper.

BUSINESS DEPARTMENT: Gets advertisements and is in charge of distribution of the paper.

MECHANICAL DEPARTMENT: Decides where the articles, pictures, and ads will go and then prints the paper.

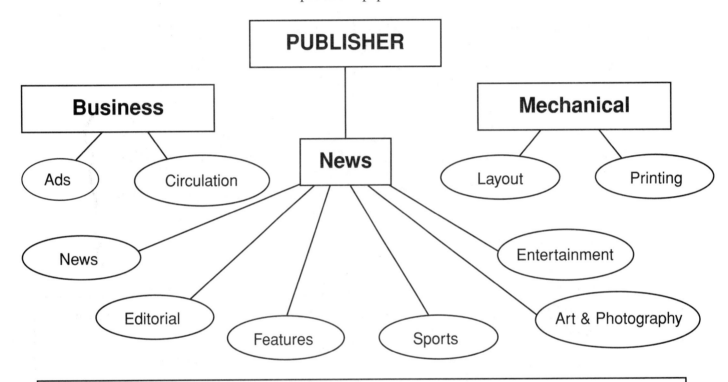

You are the Publisher of the paper. To which departments will you assign the following work? Write Business, News, or Mechanical on each line.

1. _____ write a story about a shipwreck

2. _____ get a large store to run an ad for their sale

3. _____ decide where the ad should go

4. _____ draw an illustration for a science article

FIND THE FOLLOWING IN A NEWSPAPER:

- *a page with stories, photos, and art*
- *three different kinds of articles*
- *an advertisement*

Challenge: Find the name of the paper's publisher and/or editor-in-chief.

THE NEWS DEPARTMENT

The *News Department* is led by an editor in chief. This department must write and illustrate all the articles and features that appear in the paper. The department is divided into sections according to types of articles. The following are among the sections most likely to be found in a large newspaper: NEWS, EDITORIAL, FEATURES, SPORTS, ENTERTAINMENT, ART and PHOTOGRAPHY.

You are the Editor in Chief of the News Department. To which section of your department will you give the following assignments?

1. _____cover the big basketball game
2. _____write a story about a plane crash
3. _____take a photo of the crash
4. _____write an editorial opinion about an election
5. _____see a play and write a review of it
6. _____write a feature story about cooking with apples

FIND THE FOLLOWING IN A NEWSPAPER:

- *a news article and a sports story*
- *a news photograph*
- *an example of newspaper artwork*
- *an editorial*

THE NEWS SECTION

The *News Section* of the News Department is made up of the news editor and news reporters. The job of the reporters is to write news articles and headlines for the paper. The editor of the *News Section* assigns a reporter to write an article or story. Reporters sometimes work cooperatively to provide background information, conduct interviews, or write headlines and articles.

You are the News Editor. For tomorrow's paper you must have three articles for the front page. These should be the most important stories of the day. Here is a list of events to which you must send reporters. Check the three that you think are front page material so that you can send your best reporters.

- ☐ a dog show
- ☐ a cooking contest
- ☐ a volcanic eruption
- ☐ a big airplane crash
- ☐ a visit from a queen
- ☐ an oil spill
- ☐ new rules about pollution control
- ☐ the president's speech

On the back of this paper tell why you chose the ones you did.

FIND THREE FRONT PAGE STORIES IN A NEWSPAPER.

Cut them out including their headlines. Cut the headlines from the articles. Work in small groups. Put the headlines in one pile and the stories in another. Mix them up. Each group member should draw three headlines and three articles. Take turns reading an article aloud. See who has the matching headline.

THE EDITORIAL SECTION

Another section of the News Department is the **Editorial Section.** The writers in this section write opinions about the news instead of just facts. Their articles are called editorials.

The editorial page of a newspaper may also include an editorial cartoon (an opinion expressed in cartoon fashion) and letters to the editor (opinions written by readers of the paper).

FACT = NEWS

OPINION = EDITORIAL

Read the following statement pairs. Write F-N on the line if it is a fact which should be reported in the news or O-E, if it is an opinion which should be written in an editorial.

1. _____The air in Big City is very polluted.

2. _____Laws should be passed to control automobile pollution.

3. _____The town's most dangerous intersection needs a traffic signal.

4. _____Two cars crashed at the corner of Fifth and Main.

5. _____The United States should send aid to the rebels in Central America.

6. _____Fighting between the government and rebels continues in Central America.

7. _____There are 3,000 homeless people in Big City.

8. _____All homeless people should be forced to go to shelters in the winter.

WRITE YOUR *OPINION* ABOUT ONE OF THE FOLLOWING:
- *Smoking in public places*
- *Deposits on soda cans*
- *Bikes and skateboards on sidewalks*
- *Loud radios in public places*

FIND AND CUT OUT THE FOLLOWING IN A NEWSPAPER:
- *The editorial page*
- *An editorial cartoon*
- *A letter to the editor*

THE FEATURE SECTION

The News Department also includes a *Feature Section*. Feature writers choose subjects for stories that will interest the newspaper's readers.

Feature articles may be about people, travel, cooking, organizations, gardening, decorating, new products, etc. Features may require a lot of research and take a long time to prepare.

List four important people who might have a feature written about them. Find out about one of them and write a paragraph.

List four places you might like to travel to. Choose one, research it, and write why a tourist would want to go there.

List four foods you would like recipes for. Find and copy a recipe, including directions, for one of them.

List four other feature articles that you might like to read in a newspaper. Research one of them and write a paragraph about it.

FIND THE FOLLOWING IN A NEWSPAPER:

- *a feature story about a person*

Read the article.

On a separate piece of paper, write what you learned about the person.

THE SPORTS SECTION

The **Sports Section** covers current sporting events and people. This section usually works on a "beat" system. This means that a reporter is assigned to a particular sport and covers only stories that have to do with it.

The **Sports Section** may have beats for football, baseball, basketball, tennis, golf, hockey, etc.

YOU HAVE JUST BEEN HIRED AS A REPORTER FOR THE SPORTS SECTION. You must complete the following form so your editor can assign you to a beat.

BEAT ASSIGNMENT APPLICATION

What is your favorite sport? _____

Why? _____

_____

_____

Name at least two heroes in your sport. _____

_____

Why are they considered heroes? _____

_____

_____

FIND THE FOLLOWING IN A NEWSPAPER:

- *articles about four different sports*

Work in small groups to make a sports' scrapbook. Organize the scrapbook by grouping like sports together. Label the articles "game" if it's about a particular game and "person" if it's about a sports personality. Did your group find any articles that don't fit in either category? If so, add another classification.

THE ENTERTAINMENT SECTION

If you want to know what's on TV, at the movies, the name of a good book, or something about your favorite star, you car look in the **Entertainment Section** of a newspaper.

This section is all about fun. It may include puzzles and comic strips. To help their readers make choices about what to do, the reporters in this section write reviews. Reviews are the reporter's opinion of a book, a movie, or a performance. When reading reviews, you must keep in mind that your opinion may be different from the reviewer's.

MOVIE SCHEDULE

ABC Theaters

Center City

9th & Chestnut
946-0031

Forward to the Past
12:00	2:00
4:00	6:00
8:00	

The Big Deal
12:30	2:30
4:30	6:30
8:30	

Suburban

901 N, Main
896-0001

Little One
11:30	3:30
5:30	7:30
9:30	

Scary Nights
8:00	10:00
12:00	

Fletcher's Flicks

Fletcher's Flicks IV

8th & Walnut
831-9000

Move Over Rover
11:20	2:15
5:10	8:20
10:30	

Mickey's Mouse
10:00	12:00
2:00	4:00
6:00	8:00

Monday Madness
1:00	4:00
8:00	10:00

Good News Gnus
6:00	7:45
9:45	11:45

Movies by Samco

Samco I

Main at 6th
896-6000

Forward to the Past
11:00	1:00
3:00	5:00
7:00	9:00

Good News Gnus
12:00	2:00
4:00	6:30
8:00	10:00

Samco II

Olive Mall
658-2888

Oh, Bermuda!
3:00	5:00
8:00	

Call of the Owl
2:00	4:00
6:00	9:00
11:00	

Samco III

1000 State Highway
457-0101

Uncle Duck
10:00	12:00
2:00	4:00
6:00	8:00

Moving West
11:30	1:30
3:30	5:30
7:30	9:30

Vacation in Paradise
10:45	12:45
2:45	4:45
6:45	8:45

Seashores
12:15	2:15
4:15	6:15
8:15	

Use the schedule above to answer these questions:

1. At what theaters could you see *Forward to the Past?* _____

   _____

2. If you want to see *Good News Gnus* right after lunch, where should you go?_____

3. It is 5:00. You live 10 minutes from Samco III. You want to see a movie right away. Which movie will you see? _____

4. You live on Main Street. Which theaters are probably close to you? _____

   _____

FIND THE FOLLOWING IN A NEWSPAPER:

- *an article about a famous performer or artist*
- *a movie, play, or performance review*
- *a comic strip*
- *a puzzle*

PHOTOGRAPHY

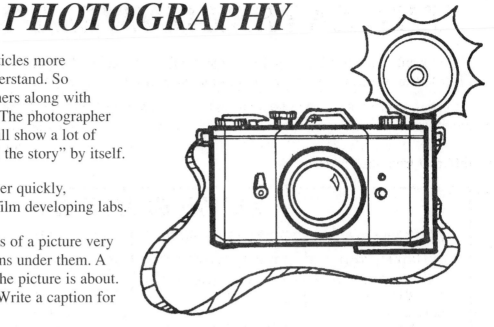

Pictures make newspaper articles more interesting and easier to understand. So newspapers send photographers along with reporters to cover the news. The photographer tries to take a picture that will show a lot of action. It should almost "tell the story" by itself.

To use the picture in the paper quickly, newspapers have their own film developing labs.

In order to make the contents of a picture very clear, newspapers put captions under them. A caption tells who and what the picture is about. Look at the pictures below. Write a caption for each.

Caption: _____
_____
_____
_____

Caption: _____
_____
_____
_____

Caption: _____
_____
_____
_____

Caption: _____
_____
_____
_____

NEWSPAPER ART

Sometimes a picture is needed that cannot be taken with a camera. For example, a story may need a diagram, graph, or map to make it clear. Artists must produce these drawings quickly to meet the deadline for printing the paper. Artists may also create graphics for advertisements, comic strips, political cartoons, etc.

Join with 3 or 4 classmates. YOU ARE THE ARTISTS FOR A NEWSPAPER. Here are your assignments for the day. Divide them among your group. Do the necessary research (encyclopedias are good) and make the needed drawings.

A volcano has erupted on Hawaii. Make a diagram of the interior of a volcano to illustrate how a volcano works.

Make a picture of a car for the automobile section.

Draw a map of Iowa to show where Des Moines is located, the scene of a plane crash.

Make an enlarged diagram of a fruit fly to show the insect that is ruining the orange crop

Make a bar or line graph that shows that the average temperature in January was 15°, in February 20°, in March 45°, in April 60°, in May 75°, in June 75°, July 85°, August 80°, September 70°, October 65°, November 45° December 20°—for an article on the changing weather.

Make a circle graph to show that $1/2$ of the people surveyed want a new train system, $1/4$ do not, and $1/4$ are undecided.

Draw a picture of a teddy bear for a toy store ad.

FIND THE FOLLOWING IN A NEWSPAPER:

- *a news photograph that "tells a story."*
- *a sports photograph that shows action*
- *a diagram, map, or graph done by an artist*
- *an example of art in an advertisement*
- *a comic strip or political cartoon done by an artist*

THE BUSINESS DEPARTMENT-CIRCULATION SECTION

The job of the **Business Department** is to make sure the newspaper makes money. One of the ways a newspaper earns income is by selling papers. The circulation manager is in charge of distribution. A paper can be delivered by carrier or mail. Many people also buy newspapers at newsstands or from vending machines.

Use information from the pictures above to solve these problems.

1. How much does home delivery cost per day? _____

2. How much would it cost to buy a paper every day for one 30 day month with 4 Sundays at JOE'S NEWS?_____

   How much would you save by having the paper delivered at home? _____

3. How much would it cost to buy the paper at the vending machine for a 30 day, 4 Sunday month? _____

   How much would you save by having the paper delivered at home? _____

Challenge

4. Why is home delivery so much cheaper? _____

FIND THE FOLLOWING ABOUT A NEWSPAPER:

- *How much does it cost on a weekday?* _____ *Sunday?*_____

- *How much does home delivery cost?*_____

ADVERTISING

A newspaper makes most of its money by selling advertising space. A full-page ad may cost thousands of dollars. An advertising manager is in charge of getting businesses to use the paper for advertisements. The sales staff must convince business people that the ad will increase their business since so many readers will see it. Once a company has decided to advertise in the paper, the advertising department's artists may help the business develop an ad that will catch people's attention and get them to buy their product.

Ad 1

SNEAKER SALE

Regular
$65.95

Now $39.95

Ad 2

BILL'S SPORT SHOP SNEAKER SALE

Regular $65.95
Now $39.95

Get them while they last!

22 N. Main Street
Big City
Call 101-0001 for more information

Ad 3

BIG SNEAKER SALE

at

BILL'S SPORT SHOP

*22 N. Main Street
Big City*

Regular $65.95
Now $39.95

Sat. & Sun. Only 9 am-9 pm each day

Call 101-0001 for more information.

1. Which ad "catches your eye"?_____

2. Which ad(s) tells you where to buy the product? _____

3. Which ad(s) tells you the store's hours? _____

4. Which ad(s) gives you information that would help you if you wanted to ask some questions? ___

5. Which do you think is the best ad? _____

FIND THE FOLLOWING IN A NEWSPAPER:

- *four different sizes of ads*
- *an ad with art in it*
- *an ad that uses photographs*
- *an ad that is mostly words*

CLASSIFIED ADVERTISING

A newspaper has a section where people can place short ads. It is called the **Classified Advertising Section** because the ads are classified, or organized. They can be For Sale, Help Wanted, Lost and Found, etc. Classified ads are usually phoned in to a paper. The operators who answer the phone must be able to help callers compose their ads and get them into the right classification. Since classified ads are usually paid for by the line, all the necessary information must be given in as few words as possible.

Here is an example:

> ## HELP WANTED
> Paper carrier for West Hill.
> 7 days a week. Early am.
> Call Sue at 565-4329 for info.

YOU ARE A CLASSIFIED AD OPERATOR.

Below are two calls that you received. Write the ad which will appear in the paper. Remember to include only the necessary information and make the ad as short as possible. Write them on the lines.

1. I want to sell my bike so I can get a new one. It is red and silver. It can go fast. It is a 24" boys' dirt bike. I want to sell it for $35.00. My name is John Smith. I live at 223 South Maple Street in Newtown. My phone number is 383-8383.

   _____

   _____

   _____

   _____

   _____

   _____

2. I am so sad. My dog is lost. He ran away when I opened the door and I can't find him anywhere. His name is Rex and he is a mixed breed, all black with one white paw. He's never run away before. If anyone finds him, they should bring him home to 25 Mystic Court or call me at 225-5896. I will give them a $50.00 reward. My name is Shelly Springton. Please put this ad in quickly; I miss him so much.

   _____

   _____

   _____

   _____

   _____

   _____

FIND THE FOLLOWING IN A NEWSPAPER:
- *Help Wanted ad*
- *Lost and Found ad*
- *For Sale ad*

THE MECHANICAL DEPARTMENT—TYPESETTING

The work of all the other departments and sections come together in the printing of the newspaper. This is the job of the **Mechanical Department.** All of the stories, art, and photos must be *typeset*—put into a form for printing. This is a big job. Most modern papers use computers to help them.

CHOOSING THE FONT

One of the decisions that must be made before printing is what kind of type—the **font**—will be used. A font is a combination of three things—*typeface, type size,* and *type weight.*

TYPEFACE

The style of type is called *typeface*. For example, letters may have *serifs*—small extra horizontal lines.

M ⟵ SERIFS ⟶ B

Or, they may be *sans-serif*, without extra lines.

M   SANS-SERIFS   B

Some common typefaces are Times Roman (serif), Helvetica (sans-serif), and *Zapf Chancery* (script).

TYPE SIZE

Type may be LARGE, small, or many other sizes. *Type size* is measured in points. One point is very small. Most of the type on this page is 12 point.

TYPE WEIGHT

Type weight is the thickness and slant of the lines in letters. For example, words may be printed in **boldface**, with a fine line, in *italics*, or in combinations like ***bold italics.***

TRY THIS:

Cut two or more headlines from a newspaper. Copy them onto a piece of paper so you won't forget what they say. Then cut the letters apart. Mix them up. Now reassemble the headlines. Line the letters up straight. This is something like the job typesetters had before machines were invented to help them. Imagine doing this for a whole newspaper!

FIND THE FOLLOWING IN NEWSPAPERS:

- *three different typefaces*
- *several sizes of type*
- *examples of bold,* fine, *and italic print*

LAYOUT

Deciding where the stories, pictures, ads, etc. will go is called *layout*. Someone must "lay out" the parts of a page to see where they will fit and look good. The arrangement is then glued to a sheet the size of the newspaper's page. This is called the paste up.

Cut on the dark lines on this page and the next. Arrange the pieces on two papers this size and "paste them up." Draw appropriate pictures or ads for the empty spaces. Compare your arrangement with others. Are they alike?

By George Scott

NEW CITY—Students were overjoyed today when the city schools closed for summer vacation. At 12:00 noon the children left the schools on their way to vacations, swimming, ball games, and all the other pleasures of the long-awaited summer.

At Glenwood School 285 joyful youngsters met in the school auditorium for one last sing-a-long just before school was dismissed. The favorite song was "In the Good Old Summertime."

Later, Jeremy Holmes was dejected as he waited for his bus. "You'd think it could be on time today of all days!" he exclaimed.

MANY CHILDREN HEAD FOR PARKSIDE POOL

HEADLINE

SCHOOL is OUT!

BANNER

By Juanita Lopez

NEW CITY—During the morning of June 22, the last day of school for New City youngsters, Principal Mary Jones visited each class to wish the children a happy and safe summer vacation. Ever the educator, she also encouraged them to read and write over the summer. "It's fun and you'll remember what you've learned for next fall," said Jones.

By Lee Chang

NEW CITY—Five hundred fifty city children crowded Parkside Pool on Friday afternoon after city schools were dismissed for vacation. "It could be a long, hot summer," said weary lifeguard, John Stewart.

SUMMER VACATION BEGINS

SUBHEAD

PRINCIPAL JONES VISITS CLASSES TO SAY GOOD-BYE

HEADLINE

LAYOUT *(cont.)*

The layout person must be very familiar with all parts of a newspaper.

- **MASTHEAD** – *Goes across the top of the front page. Tells the name of the paper, where it is printed, and the date of the issue.*
- **LOG**–*A slogan, design, or artwork that is the paper's trademark.*
- **HEADLINE**–*The large words above a story which introduce it.*
- **BANNER**—*The main headline on page 1 which tells about the main story of the day.*
- **SUBHEAD**–*A small headline which gives more information about a story.*
- **BY-LINE**–*Tells who wrote the story.*
- **DATELINE**–*Tells where the story happened.*
- **CAPTION**—*The words under a picture that tell about it.*
- **COPY**—*All the words in a paper.*
- **INDEX**—*A table of contents for the paper, usually found on the front page.*

THE GLENWOOD
SCHOOL TIMES

New City   *June 22, 20___*

LOGO

MASTERHEAD

VACATION PLANS

HEADLINE

Students leave Glenwood School and head for summer vacation.

CAPTION

INDEX

Classified............4
Comics...............4
Editorial.............2
Features 3
News..............1, 2
Reviews 4
Sports 3
Weather..............2

By Sky Lightfoot

BY-LINE

NEW CITY—

DATELINE

When asked about their vacation plans, Glenwood students reported a wide range of activities. Tommy Slater plans to add to his snake collection on his trips to the woods. Mary Smith is flying to Hawaii with her family. She wants to see a volcano. Juan Carlos will visit his grandmother in Mexico. Paula McCay plans to sit on her porch swing and read, read, read. It sounds like a relaxing, fun summer.

PRINTING

The paste ups are used to make printing plates which are curved to fit on a large cylinder of a printing press. Paper from huge rolls is pulled through the presses to print the paper in much the same way paper rolls through a typewriter. This happens at a very high speed. Other machines cut and fold the pages.

YOU CAN PRINT FROM A CYLINDER

Assemble these materials:

card board tube(s)from paper towels or wraps

heavy string

water

white glue

spoon or stirrer

scissors

waxed paper and foil

small dish or foil pan

tempera paints or colored ink

cookie sheet with sides

paper on which to print

Follow these directions:

1. Thin white glue with a little water in the dish. Stir until well mixed.

2. Cut the string into short lengths.

3. Dip each piece of string in the glue mixture making sure it is completely wet.

4. Glue the string onto the cardboard tube in an interesting picture or design. Leave the ends of the tube free to use as "handles." (If you wish to make letters, they must be backwards in order to print correctly. A good way to do this is to write with dark marker on a thin piece of paper. Turn the paper over and copy what shows through to the reverse side.)

5. Put the tube on waxed paper to dry.

6. Line the cookie sheet with foil. Spread some tempera paint or ink in a thin layer.

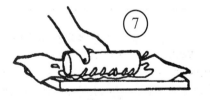

7. Roll the dried tube in the paint until the string is inked.

8. Now roll the tube on your paper to see your print. Hint: You can let your tube dry and then add to your print with another color or you can make a tube for each color you wish to use.

USING THE INDEX

You want to know tomorrow's weather so you can plan what to wear. You know it's in the newspaper, but where? Use the index to find out!

Large newspapers are divided into sections which are lettered at the top of the page. Then the pages are numbered within each section. So, the page number may be B 3—meaning section B, page 3

Use the index above to decide what page(s) might help you answer these questions.

INDEX

Classified Ads	F 1-8
Comics	E 6-8
Editorials	B 7-8
Food	D1-4
Letters to the Editor	B 7
Local News	B1-4
Movie & TV Schedules	E5
National News	A 1-8
People	D 7-8
Puzzles	E8
Reviews	E 1-4
Sports	C1-8
Travel	D 5-6
Weather	E 7
World News	A 1-8

Question   **Page (s)**

1. Will I need a jacket tomorrow? _____

2. Is there a second-hand dirt bike for sale? _____

3. Has anyone found my lost ring? _____

4. How strong was the earthquake in Japan? _____

5. What movie is playing at Eastern Theater? _____

6. Is there an article on my favorite rock star? _____

7. Who won the football game? _____

8. Is the play at the Bijou worth seeing? _____

9. Where should I go on my summer vacation? _____

10. What should I fix for dinner? _____

11. Was the mayor of our town reelected? _____

12. Was Jason's letter complaining about litter in the park published? _____

13. What time does tonight's TV movie begin? _____

14. What is my favorite cartoon character doing today? _____

15. Can I solve today's crossword puzzle? _____

16. What did the president say about Europe? _____

17. What opinion does this paper have about the proposed path of the new highway? _____

18. Are there any golf tournaments being played this weekend? _____

BE A NEWSPAPER DETECTIVE!

Can you spy these parts of a newspaper? As you find them, check them off on the list below. Then cut them out and place them in an envelope stapled to this paper or a scrapbook. You may have to look in several issues. Don't forget to use the index when you can!

Find these:

By-line of a woman reporter	Article about a place to visit	Recipe you'd like to try
Dateline from a foreign country	Caption mentioning an animal. (Include the picture, too.)	Word Puzzle
Classified ad for a guitar or bike for sale	Article mentioning a holiday	Advertisement for computers
Dateline from another city in your country	Article with headline and subhead	Graph, diagram, map, or other art which illustrates a story.
Headline about the president or prime minister	Humorous headline	Classified ad for a lost dog
Classified ad for a job you might like when you grow up	Sports photo	By-line of a man reporter
Headline about a sports event	Full-page ad	Article about a famous person (news or feature)
Funny cartoon or comic strip	Weather map	Sports photograph showing action

READING WEATHER MAPS

Weather maps appear in many daily newspapers. They are usually based on information received from the National Weather Service. They show conditions at a certain time and date. And, they predict the high and low temperatures for that day in selected cities.

SYMBOLS

Rain

Snow

49/32   High & Low Daily Temperature (°F)

○ Clear Skies

◑ Party Cloudy

● Cloudy

▲ Cold Front

●— Warm Front

WEATHER MAP

Winnipeg 28/10
Montreal 43/36
Boise 40/27
Cheyenne 30/25
Chicago 49/32
New York City 58/42
Los Angeles 70/53
Albuquerque 64/35
Houston 80/58
Atlantic Ocean
Miami 79/70

Use the weather map and symbols above to answer these questions.

1. Name two cities where it is raining. _____

2. Name two cities where it is snowing. _____

3. Will you need a winter coat in Los Angeles on this day?_____

4. Name two states (you may have to use a United States map for help) that have a cold front moving through them. _____

5. Which country has more snow on this day—Canada or United States?_____

6. What are the predicted high and low temperatures for

   Chicago? _____

   Albuquerque? _____

   Winnipeg? _____

   Montreal? _____

7. What is the symbol for cloudy weather?_____

8. You are flying to Chicago today; what special weather gear will you need?_____

   _____

9. Would this be a good day for a trip to Disney World? _____

10. What is the weather like today in your area? _____

WRITING NEWS STORIES

You are a reporter who has been assigned to cover the new mandatory recycling program in your city. Check the ones you might do.

1. _____ Interview the mayor and council members to find out why they made recycling mandatory.

2. _____ Study file stories regarding the planning and development of the recycling plan.

3. _____ Go to the library to read about the history of recycling.

4. _____ Talk to the local garbage collection and landfill operators to find out why a recycling program is necessary.

5. _____ Include your opinion about recycling in the article.

6. _____ Take a photographer to the new recycling center to get a picture of it in operation.

7. _____ Interview the manager of the recycling center.

8. _____ Ask an artist to draw a diagram showing the steps in recycling an aluminum can.

9. _____ Interview city residents to see how they feel about recycling.

10. _____ Write the story without checking to see if the facts are accurate.

A REPORTER'S BEST FRIENDS

A reporter must make sure that all the important information is included in a news story. There are questions that will help organize this information. They can be used as an outline or guide for taking notes and writing.

The 5 W's (WHO, WHAT, WHEN, WHERE, WHY) and HOW can be a reporter's best friends!

Read the sentences from news stories below. Write one of the 5 W's or HOW to tell which question the bold part of the sentence answers. The first has been done for you.

WHO is the story about?
WHAT happened?
WHEN did it happen?
WHERE did it happen?
WHY did it happen?
HOW did it happen?

WHO 1. **Mrs. Smith, the school librarian,** helped them organize special activities for National Book Week.

_____ 2. They held a **Favorite Book Celebration.**

_____ 3. National Book Week is **November 13-17** this year.

_____ 4. The children in Room 8 decided to celebrate Book Week **because they like to read so much.**

_____ 5. All the classes in Fernwood Elementary School participated in a Favorite Characters Parade **on the school playgrounds.**

_____ 6. The principal organized the classes **by grade level** for the parade.

Write six sentences of your own to illustrate the question words. Circle the part that answers the question.

WHO: _____

_____

WHAT: _____

_____

WHEN: _____

_____

WHERE: _____

_____

WHY: _____

_____

HOW: _____

_____

FIND THE FACTS

A news story gives readers the facts by answering the questions WHO, WHAT, WHEN, WHERE, WHY, and HOW. Read the story below to find the Five W's and HOW. List them below.

The OAKWOOD SCHOOL TIMES

VOLCANO CAUSES SCHOOL FIRE

Eastown—A small fire was quickly extinguished in Miss Nelson's fifth grade classroom on Wednesday.

The fire began during a demonstration of a model volcano built by a group of students. Fortunately, the demonstrators were prepared for just such an emergency and fast action with a bottle of water prevented a school-wide emergency.

The model papier-mache volcano was supposed to be covered with plaster of Paris to make it fireproof. However, a small section of exposed paper was concealed by the paint covering the model. This ignited when the hot ashes created by the

Miss Sharon Nelson and students, Jan Smith and Sam Brown, show volcano that almost caused school fire.

chemical used to erupt the volcano realistically spewed down the mountainside.

"It's important to be prepared," commented Teacher Nelson. "I plan to screen science projects more closely in the future."

WHO _____

WHAT _____

WHEN _____

WHERE _____

WHY _____

HOW _____

TAKING NOTES

Since a news story is built around the 5 W's and HOW, a reporter can use them to organize the notes from which he will write his story.

Use the following form to take notes for a news story. Report on a happening at your school or use one of the PRACTICES on the next page.

NOTES FOR _____ *STORY*

DATE:

WHO:
WHAT:

WHEN:
WHERE:

WHY:

HOW:

DETAILS:

WRITING LEADS

A good news story starts with a strong **LEAD** sentence(s). A lead is so interesting that it leads the reader on to the rest of the story.

As many of the Five W's and HOW as are necessary to summarize the story are included in the lead sentence(s). Often only the **What**, **Who**, and **When** or **Where** are in the lead. **Why** and **How** provide details for the rest of the story.

A reporter will usually start the lead with the Who or What depending on whether the person or the event is more important. The point is made in as few words as possible without missing essential information.

EXAMPLES:

WHAT	**WHO**	**WHEN**

An extra vacation day has been added to Spring Break, R.F. Dunlap, Principal, announced today.

WHO	**WHAT**	**WHEN**

Beverly Meyers, sixth grader, was voted Student Council President in yesterday's election.

WHAT	**WHEN**	**WHERE**

Deck the halls with sneezing, coughing, and sniffles! Sixty new cases of flu were reported the week before Christmas at Lincoln School.

PRACTICE WRITING LEADS

Use the facts below or your notes from the previous page. Remember, the lead will not include all of the 5 W's and HOW.

1. Party
   Sponsored by 6th
   Grade
   School clothes
   Disco music
   Friday, January 10
   Cafeteria
   7:30 p.m.
   Theme: "Winter
   Fun"
   To raise money for
   homeless people
   Admission: $5.00
   Parents donating
   food.

2. Bus added
   No more crowding
   No more waiting
   Ed Miller,
   transportation
   director,
   announced
   Sleepy Hollow route
   Starting Monday,
   December 6
   School Board
   approved
   purchase at
   November
   meeting.

3. Dog
   Entered open door
   Runs through
   Mission School
   Disrupts classes
   Belongs to fourth
   grader, Bob
   Scanlon
   Monday
   Nips gym teacher
   Barks at principal
   Caught by dog
   catcher
   Bob, "I guess Spot
   wondered where I
   was."

THE WHOLE STORY

The Lead Paragraph

The lead sentence should merge smoothly into the rest of the first paragraph of your story. Add the next most important fact after the lead or explain in more detail one of the facts given in the lead. Be sure to cover the 5 W's and HOW.

Fill in the blanks below to complete this lead paragraph about a school carnival.

On Saturday, May 5, North Elementary Glee Club will turn the playground into the biggest carnival seen in years.

_____ , the club's president,
said the purpose for having this_____
is not only to raise money for their trip to _____ but
to promote school spirit. Members of the club hope all school families
will enjoy this fun activity.

Rest of Article

The other paragraphs of the article should fill in more details about the Glee Club and its carnival.

On the lines below, list some details that could be used in the other paragraphs. Use your imagination.

   A. Details about the carnival.

      1 _____

      2. _____

      3. _____

   B. Details about the Glee Club. (Purpose and reason for trip)

      1. _____

      2. _____

      3. _____

   C. Membership of the club.

      1. _____

      2. _____

      3. _____

On a separate piece of paper, copy the lead paragraph above. Then use your lists to write the complete Glee Club article. (See page 29 for writing suggestions.)

ON YOUR OWN

Use your notes from the form on page 26 to write a complete news article.

These suggestions may help you:

Each paragraph should contain only one main idea. To help each paragraph blend into the next, you can do the following things:

1. Repeat a key word from the previous paragraph.

2. Use a synonym that refers to a key word from the previous paragraph.

   Example: If the key word was *gigantic*, you can use the word *enormous*.

3. Refer to a fact from the previous paragraph, or use the adjectives this and that, or the pronouns, he, she, and it to refer to someone or something from the previous paragraph.

4. Use connective words like: another, obviously, also, furthermore, first, next, for example, therefore, moreover, further, hence, for instance, etc.

Think of your news story as an upside down triangle. The most important part is at the top of the article and each following paragraph tells less important facts.

LEAD PARAGRAPH

Rest of the very important information.

Next most important information.

Least significant Information.

Good luck and have fun!

PROOFREADING

The newspaper staff proofreads an article several times before it is sent to the printers.

Proofreading is very important, because a newspaper with errors is embarrassing and looks messy.

Proofreading marks, or corrections, are made in the margins. The word or words to be changed are circled.

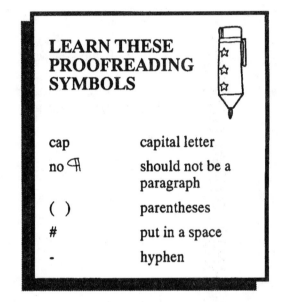

LEARN THESE PROOFREADING SYMBOLS

cap	capital letter
no ¶	should not be a paragraph
( )	parentheses
#	put in a space
-	hyphen

Directions:

Re-write the following sentences making the necessary corrections.

1. The snowstorm on Friday lasted three (three) days.   *ℓ*

2. (traffic) was at a stand still for over an hour○───○•   *cap*

3. There are (200) students in the cafe.   *spell*

4. Helen her sisters and her mother went to visit (mr.) Hill.   *cap* ○,

5. Where is he what is he doing○───○?   *and*

6. (¶) I like Mary she doesn't wear make-up said Mark. "
○,

7. Was Mr. (smith) the last (pasenger) to leave?   *spell*
(cap)

8. She was born in (minnespolis, minnesota).   *cap*

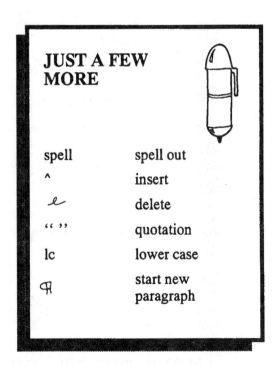

JUST A FEW MORE

spell	spell out
^	insert
ℓ	delete
" "	quotation
lc	lower case
¶	start new paragraph

PROOFREADING *(cont.)*

Directions:

Your turn to proofread.

Use the proofreading symbols (see page 30).

1. For three year I would to to the country for the summer

2. the driver rode all day long

3. She walked out onto stagge.

4. Jan bathed her dog and he brother play with the ball.

5. No you can not go outside said Henry.

6. She picked 14 girls for the cheerleading squad.

7. we plan on taking our vacation in florida next year.

8. The zoo was a noisy exciting wonderful place to visit.

9. Worms like to stay in the dirt. it is dark and damp.

10. Wen i grew up i want to a report or.

Proofread your own or a partner's article.

HEADLINES

Headline is the word for the title of a newspaper article. It should tell you the most important information in the lead paragraph. It is the briefest summary of the news story. The reader should know what's in the story after reading the headline.

Headlines should be as interesting as possible while describing the content of the story.

Reporters often try to make their headlines "catchy."

POINTS TO REMEMBER:

1. Treat a headline like a complete sentence; it should have a subject and a verb.

2. Eliminate the use of "the," "an," and "a" in a headline.

3. A headline does not require a period at the end.

4. A headline should catch the reader's eye.

5. Use short, crisp words that are lively and colorful.

6. Capitalize all important words.

STUDYING HEADLINES

Find four headlines with words in them that you don't know. Cut them out.

Fold a piece of plain paper in half the long way. Use the paper with the opening at the bottom and the fold at the top. Glue a headline on the front. Write " In Other Words " in the lower right hand corner. Using a dictionary, look up the word(s) you don't know. On the inside write what the headline means. Do this for your other headlines.

Exchange headlines with your classmates. See if you know what their headlines mean.

Find four "catchy" headlines. Fold paper as above and attach the headline. Write "It's catchy because..." in the lower right hand corner. Inside tell what makes this headline catchy. Share with your classmates.

Now write a headline for the article you have written.

FROM THE HORSE'S MOUTH

Reporters often use interviews to collect information for their articles. By talking directly to a person who knows about the subject, a reporter can get his facts straight "from the horse's mouth," as the old saying goes.

Match the information in the left column with the person who was interviewed in the right box. Write the correct letter in the blank.

_____ 1. The band concert will start at 7:30 p.m. on Wednesday.

_____ 2. A student was injured in a playground accident.

_____ 3. Student art will be displayed in the hallways.

_____ 4. Soccer will be a new sport offered next year.

_____ 5. New buses will arrive on Tuesday.

_____ 6. An all-school assembly is scheduled for next Friday.

_____ 7. The chorus will meet for extra practice at 8:00 a.m. every Monday.

_____ 8. The lunch menu has been changed for next week.

_____ 9. The fourth grades will perform plays they have written.

_____ 10. An activity night for sixth graders will be sponsored by the parent's organization.

a. Coach Jones

b. transportation director

c. playground aide

d. Principal Mitchell

e. music teacher

f. cafeteria manager

g. fourth grade teacher

h. band director

i. president of parent group

j. art teacher

INTERVIEWS

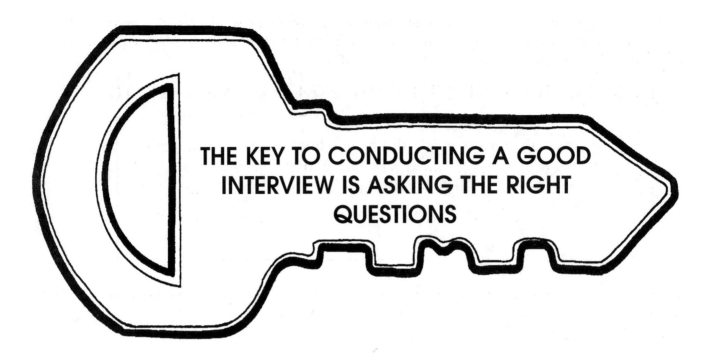

THE KEY TO CONDUCTING A GOOD INTERVIEW IS ASKING THE RIGHT QUESTIONS

Before conducting an interview, a reporter should have his questions prepared and written down. The list of questions can start with the 5 W's and HOW. Questioning continues by asking the person being interviewed to elaborate on (tell more about) the Why, How, and Who.

Choose a character from a book you have read. Write questions for the character. Then write what you think their answer would be if you could interview them. Be creative! This is fun if you use familiar characters from fairy tales, tall tales, or common children's literature.

Who _____ **?**

Answer: _____

What _____ **?**

Answer: _____

When _____ **?**

Answer: _____

Where _____ **?**

Answer: _____

Why _____ **?**

Answer: _____

How _____ **?**

Answer: _____

DIRECT QUOTES

A person being interviewed may express an opinion or say something so well that the reporter will want to include the person's actual words in the story. This is called a ***direct quote***. It must be punctuated correctly and the person who said it must be identified.

CIRCLE THE DIRECT QUOTE BELOW. UNDERLINE WHO SAID IT.

> Several students at Worthington School enjoyed participating in a drill program called, The Mad Minute. They further stated that the daily drill helped improve their math skills. Rosa Phillipe enjoyed the drills so much, she said, "We need to do this every day."

If you plan to use direct quotes, you must write down exactly what the person says during an interview. You may have to ask them to repeat something until you have it correct. When you write your story, use correct punctuation for the quotations.

 **Quotation marks enclose what people say.**

Quotations are separated from the rest of the sentence by a comma, unless the rest of the sentence follows a quote ending with an exclamation point or question mark.

"I like computers," said Tom.

"I love computers! " exclaimed Tom.

Tom said, " I love computers."

"Do you like computers?" asked Tom.

DIRECTIONS:

1. Write some questions that you could use to interview several of your classmates. The topic for your interview is "Computers . . . Are They Taking Over?" (Remember the Five W's and How).

2. Interview several of your classmates using your questions.

3. Write a news article telling what your classmates think. Use direct quotes and correct punctuation.

4. Add a headline.

GUIDELINES FOR INTERVIEWS

1. Make an appointment in advance. Set the time, date and place for the interview.

2. Allow enough time for the interview. Allow at least 30-45 minutes.

3. Write out your questions ahead of time. Use the Five W's & How. Ask additional questions that may occur to you during the interview.

4. Ask the questions one at a time. Write down the answers carefully.

5. If you get one word answers, ask for more explanation.

Could you tell me a little more, please?

6. Be sure to thank the person when you finish the interview. If time permits, return to interviewee with the completed article.

PRACTICE INTERVIEWING

Interview three people about their job—a family member, teacher, community worker, friend, etc. Follow the guidelines above. Then write a newspaper article about people's jobs. Use direct quotes. Add a headline.

EDITORIALS

The *editorial* is a special kind of newspaper article that includes both fact and opinion. It usually deals with a subject that causes mixed feelings. The author of the editorial tries to persuade the reader to agree with him on the issue.

Sample Editorial Page

Page 2   Thursday, November 6, 199__

THE SCHOOL TIMES
122 S. Pernell Street
Mooreside, IL 00000
Publisher:
E. Quentin Jones
Editor-in-Chief:
Theresa Smith

GIVE STUDENTS A BREAK

Lunch recess may be a thing of the past for fifth and sixth graders if the Board of Education approves the proposed change at their meeting tonight. The change was proposed by Board Member Campbell who feels that U.S. students do not spend enough time in the classroom.

Students need a break! Recess helps them learn more! Research shows that vigorous activity and fresh air following a long period of indoor inactivity, sends a fresh supply of oxygen to the brain relieving the sluggish feeling that often occurs.

The School Times urges the School Board not to eliminate recess for fifth and sixth graders. Students deserve a break and will return to the classroom refreshed and ready to get on with their learning.

LETTERS TO THE EDITOR

Dear Editor,

I think our school should get a new mascot. The lion cub is too babyish. Maybe a grown-up lion would be better. What do other people think?

Sincerely,

Jay O'Connor

The editorial page should be in the same place in each issue, located on a special inside editorial page. A small masthead replica is located on this page, which includes information about the publication and staff.

FIND THE FOLLOWING ON THE EDITORIAL PAGE ABOVE. MARK AND COLOR CODE THEM AS BELOW.

1. Name of paper (red)
2. Publisher (blue)
3. Editor-in-Chief (green)
4. Paper's address (yellow)
5. Three facts (orange)
6. Three opinions (purple)

TYPES OF EDITORIALS

There are two types of editorials written by newspaper staff—the unsigned and the signed. Unsigned editorials express the policy of the paper on different issues and are usually written by the editor in chief of the paper. Signed editorials, reflecting the opinions of the writer, are produced by other members of the editorial section.

Non-staff writers wishing to express an opinion may do so through "letters to the editor." The editor has the final word on what is printed in the newspaper so every letter received may not be included.

USE THIS OUTLINE FOR AN EDITORIAL:

I. Introduction—State the problem or issue. Tell your opinion.

II. Body—List facts, examples, and authorities that support your opinion.

III. Conclusion—Summarize your opinion and why you believe the reader should share it. Be convincing!

SPEAK OUT!

Write an editorial or letter to the editor about one of these school issues. (Take a firm stand.)

1. school lunches
2. homework
3. playground
4. grades
5. discipline
6. other (if approved by teacher)

EDITORIAL CARTOONS

Another way for opinions to be expressed in a newspaper is through an editorial cartoon. It is usually a one-picture cartoon appearing on the editorial page. It may have a short caption or speech balloons to make the opinion clear. Sometimes the editorial cartoon illustrates the editorial of the day.

Draw an editorial cartoon to illustrate an editorial you wrote.

FIND THE FOLLOWING IN A NEWSPAPER:

- *Several editorial cartoons*

Mount them on construction paper and write the opinions they express below each one. Share them with your classmates. Do they agree with your interpretation?

WRITING SPORTS STORIES

Sports writing is similar to news writing. A sports article covering a game begins with a lead containing the most important facts (remember the 5 W's and How). It continues with vivid detail describing the action of the game. A sports reporter should be able to use a wide variety of action words. The story may also contain background information about the players, coaches, game preparation, etc.

YOU ARE A SPORTS REPORTER. Use the Note-Taking Form from page 26 to organize the following information. Then write your article. Imagine you were at this exciting game. Make your readers "see" what happened. Keep them interested.

SOUTH vs. NORTH

Football Game
November 5, 2 p.m.

South scored 2 touchdowns, but missed one extra point.

North scored 3 field goals and a touchdown in the last minute of the game.

Mark Smetner, quarterback, threw the touchdown passes for South.

Jim Brown was the kicker for North.

Jerry Lee scored the winning TD.

Mark is a senior.

Jim is a junior.

Jerry is a freshman.

The game was played at Memorial Field.

This is a long-standing rivalry; both teams wanted to win badly.

North held extra practice sessions all week.

FIND IN A DAILY NEWSPAPER:
- *Ways to say one team has beaten another.*

Cut them out and mount or copy them onto a poster along with your classmate's finds. You'll be surprised at how clever sports writers are with their vocabulary.

WRITING FEATURE ARTICLES

Feature stories are written to entertain and educate the reader. Since they are not news stories, they are not written in the same way. They may be humorous or serious, but they must be based on well-researched facts. The lead in a feature story does not summarize it as it does in a news story. Instead a feature's lead should catch the readers' attention and draw them into the story.

TYPES OF FEATURE STORIES	List possible topics for each category
INFORMATIVE – educates the reader about any subject (e.g., travel, food. gardening, etc.); must be well-researched.	_____ _____ _____ _____ _____
PERSONALITY – gives a word picture of an interesting person; shown what the person is really like.	_____ _____ _____ _____ _____
EXPERIENCE OR ACCOMPLISHMENT – reports information obtained in an interview of someone who has an interesting experience or done something impressive.	_____ _____ _____ _____ _____
NEWS FEATURE – based on a current news story giving the background or human interest side.	_____ _____ _____ _____
HUMAN INTEREST – develops an emotional story from an unusual happening or situation.	_____ _____ _____ _____
MISCELLANEOUS – any other non-news entertaining, informative stories	_____ _____ _____ _____ _____

Choose one or more of your topics. Research it (conduct an interview, if necessary) and write an entertaining, informative feature article.

WRITING REVIEWS

Reviews are about an art form such as a book, play, movie, concert, art exhibit, or assembly program.

A REVIEW SHOULD:

Tell about the work of art without revealing so much that it would spoil the enjoyment of it.	**and**	**Evaluate the production by commenting knowledgeably on its quality.**

To practice writing reviews, do the following:

1. Read and review a book of your choice.

   - *Include the title, author, publisher, and where to get it*

   - *Tell enough about the book to interest others in reading it without giving away the whole story.*

   - *Evaluate the book by telling why or why not you think it a book others should read.*

   - *Be specific in in your evaluation. (Is the book good because the author tells a good story, because the characters are very believable, or because it's very funny, etc.?)*

2. Attend, then review one of the following:

Play	Band Concert
Chorus Concert	Art Exhibit
Movie	Orchestra Concert
Dance Performance	Assembly Program

- *Choose one that you feel you know about. A good reviewer is an expert in the area being reviewed.*

- *Tell something about the content of the event being reviewed.*

- *Then give your readers a specific evaluation that tells why or why not it was a good production.*

- *Comment on the performers, the setting, the choice of content, the audience reaction, etc.*

COMICS

For many people reading the daily newspaper includes reading their favorite cartoons. The characters made famous by these cartoons have become a part of our lives. Often comics teach a lesson or make a comment on life.

Cartoon characters may be animals (usually talking) or people. Once the cartoonist has planned his character, he/she must choose a situation for the character to be in, plan any other characters, and draw the characters in action. The cartoonist may draw a single picture or a strip of pictures that show a sequence of action.

Cartoonists use many tricks to make their cartoons come to life. Some of these are shown below.

NOTICE HOW THE CARTOONIST USES:

- *lines to show movement and odor*
- *three different types of "balloons" to show speech, loud sounds, and thought*
- *facial expressions and body positions to show mood and action*

YOU ARE A CARTOONIST:

Design your own character and put it into a cartoon or comic strip.

PUZZLES

Newspapers often include challenging word puzzles for their readers' entertainment. They may be crossword puzzles, word searches, or other word games.

CREATE A WORD SEARCH PUZZLE

Use the work area below.

1. Choose a topic for your puzzle—sports, foods, clothes, etc.

2. List words that the topic makes you think of.

3. Enter the words onto the grid—one letter to a box. They may go forward or backward— horizontally, vertically, or diagonally. Words with like letters may be overlapped.

4. Fill in the empty boxes with other letters all mixed up.

5. Challenge a friend to solve your word search!

My Word Search

TOPIC _____

WORD LIST

1. _____
2. _____
3. _____
4. _____
5. _____
6. _____
7. _____
8. _____
9. _____
10. _____
11. _____
12. _____

FIND THE FOLLOWING IN A NEWSPAPER:

- *3 different types of word puzzles*

PREPARING ADVERTISEMENTS

Designing newspaper ads is a specialized job. Ads may include illustrations, copy about the product (headlines, subheads, price, descriptive sentences or paragraphs), and details such as company trademark, name, and address. All of this information must be arranged into a pleasant and interesting layout.

The ad designer must keep in mind that the goal of the ad is to sell a product or service. He/she must decide which of the parts of the ad to emphasize by answering questions like these:

Is this an especially good price for the product?

Is the illustration so attractive that it would catch a reader's eye?

Is the company a well-known one whose name or trademark sells the product?

Will the customer know where to get the product?

YOU ARE AN AD DESIGNER.

Choose a product—real or imaginary. Plan the illustration, copy, and details. Then decide on a layout. Use the space below to create your ad.

WONDERFUL WORDS

Reporters must be word experts.

You can increase your word expertise by using newspapers. Keep a notebook handy (a stenographer's pad is good for this) whenever you read the newspaper. Use it to collect words and word combinations that appeal to you. Here are some ideas to start your collection.

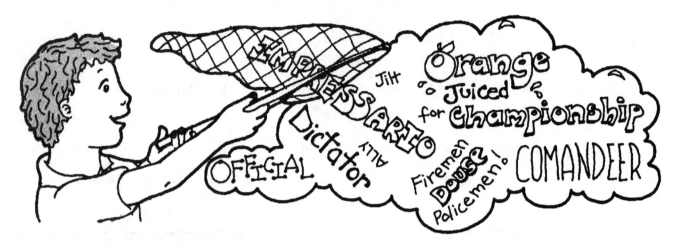

COLLECT THE FOLLOWING:

- *New vocabulary—Keep a list of words that are unfamiliar to you. Look them up in a dictionary and write their definitions next to them.*
- *Humor in words Find funny and clever word combinations in the newspaper. Headlines are a good source.*
- *Ways to say—One team beat another.*
- *Ways to say—The performance was good (or bad).*
- *Ways to say—The weather will be good (or bad).*
- *Ways to say—Said.*
- *Unusual business names—Advertisements are a good source.*
- *Clever classified ads*
- *Pun, Humorous use of words with multiple meanings.*
- *Names of comic strip characters.*
- *Name of cities and countries—especially unusual ones.*
- *Names of sports teams, professional and amateur.*
- *Shortcuts used to spell words; e.g., nite for night.*
- *Descriptive words that help you get a picture in your mind.*
- *Persuasive words used in editorials and advertisements.*
- *Funny corrections.*
- *Spelling or grammar errors.*
- *Extravagant, impressive words—advertisements are a good source.*
- *Any other words that intrigue you.*

PRACTICE ASSIGNMENTS

PERSONALITIES

Make a list of students and faculty that you could write interesting profiles about. Interview one or more and write a feature story about them.

ORGANIZATIONS

Make a list of your school's organizations. Include dates of special events connected with each one. Research (including interviews with leaders and members) one or more of them. Attend an event, if possible. Write a feature article about the organization or a review of the event.

SOCIAL EVENTS

Find out what social events will take place at your school this year. Plan to attend at least one. Write a news story announcing the event and a follow-up news story covering the event.

FADS AND FASHIONS

List current fads and fashions. Choose one or more. Find out about them. Interview users and wearers. Write a feature article about what's "in."

VOLUNTEERS

Find out which people are volunteer helpers at your school. Make arrangements to interview them. Be sure to find out why they volunteer. Write a feature story about one or more.

SPORTS

List the sports played at your school or in your community. Attend at least one game of a sport of your choice. Interview the coach and some players after the game. Write an action-packed sports story.

ANIMALS

Are there classroom pets in your school? Or, is a staff member or student noted for the animals they keep? Interview the owners and research the animal. Write an article telling others how to keep this pet.

INVESTIGATE

Are there things in your school that you wish could be changed—in the building, in the cafeteria, in the library, the curriculum, a rule or policy? Investigate to find out why things are the way they are, whether change is possible, and why change is needed. Write an editorial about at least one of them.

ANSWER KEY

Page 4
1. NEWS
2. BUSINESS
3. MECHANICAL
4. NEWS

Page 5
1. sports
2. news
3. art & photography
4. editorial
5. entertainment
6. feature

Page 6
Answers may vary.

Page 7
1. F-N
2. O-E
3. O-E
4. F-N
5. O-E
6. F-N
7. F-N
8. O-E

Page 10
1. ABC-Center City and Samco I
2. Samco I
3. Moving West
4. ABC-Suburban and Samco I

Page 13
1. $.40
2. $17.00 $5.00
3. $25.50 $13.50
4. The paper can count on the customer buying everyday.

Page 14
1. Answers may vary
2. 2 and 3
3. 3
4. 2 and 3
5. Answers will vary.

Page 20
1. E7
2. F1-8
3. F1-8
4. A1-8
5. E5
6. D7-8
7. C1-8
8. E1-4
9. D5-6
10. D1-4
11. B1-4
12. B7
13. E5
14. E6-8
15. E8
16. A1-8
17. B7-8
18. C1-8

Page 22
1. Seattle, Miami, Chicago
2. Winnipeg, Cheyenne
3. No
4. Many possible answers
5. Canada
6. Chicago 49/32
   Albuquerque 64/35
   Winnipeg 28/10
   Montreal 43/36
7. ●
8. Rain
9. No, it's raining
10. Answers will vary

Page 23
These should be checked:
1,2,3,4,6,7,8,9

Page 24
1. Who
2. What
3. When
4. Why
5. Where
6. How

Page 25
Possible answers:
Who-Miss Nelson, students
What-Fire
When-Wednesday
Where-Classroom
Why-Model was not completely covered with plaster of Paris
How-fire put out with water

Page 31
1. For three years I would go to the country for the summer.
2. The driver rode all day long.
3. She walked out onto the stage.
4. Jan bathed her dog and her brother played with the ball.
5. "No, you can not go outside," said Henry.
6. She picked fourteen girls for the cheerleading squad.
7. We plan on taking our vacation in Florida next year.
8. The zoo was a noisy, exciting, wonderful place to visit.
9. Worms like to stay in the dirt. It is dark and damp.
10. When I grow up, I want to be a reporter.

Page 33
1. h
2. c
3. j
4. a
5. b
6. d
7. e
8. f
9. g
10. i